PARALLAX

Miller Williams Poetry Series
EDITED BY PATRICIA SMITH

PARALLAX

JULIA KOLCHINSKY

THE UNIVERSITY OF ARKANSAS PRESS
FAYETTEVILLE · 2025

ISBN: 978-1-68226-268-9
eISBN: 978-1-61075-833-8

29 28 27 26 25 5 4 3 2 1

Manufactured in the United States of America

Designed by William Clift

♾ The paper used in this publication meets the minimum requirements of the American National Standard for Permanence of Paper for Printed Library Materials Z39.48-1984.

LIBRARY OF CONGRESS CATALOGING-IN-PUBLICATION DATA
Names: Kolchinsky, Julia, author.
Title: Parallax / Julia Kolchinsky.
Description: Fayetteville : The University of Arkansas Press, 2025. | Series: Miller
    Williams poetry series
Identifiers: LCCN 2024045107 (print) | LCCN 2024045108 (ebook) |
    ISBN 9781682262689 (paperback) | ISBN 9781610758338 (ebook)
Subjects: LCGFT: Poetry.
Classification: LCC PS3604.A824 P37 2025 (print) | LCC PS3604.A824 (ebook) |
    DDC 813/.6—dc23/eng/20241025
LC record available at https://lccn.loc.gov/2024045107
LC ebook record available at https://lccn.loc.gov/2024045108

For my children
& the children of my birthplace

Parallax is the apparent shift caused by viewing from two different vantage points.

Carbon, hydrogen, phosphorus, nitrogen, and oxygen are all formed inside stars. These same elements combine to form the molecules in human DNA.

CONTENTS

SERIES EDITOR'S PREFACE

Whew.

Damn. This America.

This raucous, malfunctioning, precocious, thuggish, absurdly tender, enviable, poisonous, utterly mercurial snitch of a nation. This bumptious, blustering, broken experiment. This circle of arms, haven for guns and greed, this cult of celebrity, this shelter and sanctuary, this bait for demons and demagogues. This place we call—home.

Like it or not, we're surrounded by our country. It hasn't been easy to watch its many wounds rise to the surface for anyone to see.

And maybe it's my imagination (poets are notorious for their imaginations), but I suspect more people are seeking out poetry to help with the increasingly difficult task of entering the day—screeching at Alexa to STFU, flopping out of bed, and cringing at the day's first headline.

The actual truth, assuming anyone can recognize it anymore, has been in very short supply lately. (Catch any segment of a certain cable news network for all the evidence you need.) It's not surprising that more and more neophytes are eyeing poetry's unfamiliar and untrod landscape, wondering what all the fuss has been about, also wondering if there's any semblance of truth they might stumble upon.

Longtime lovers of poetry are also on the prowl, looking for proof that they've always been savvier than everyone else, that "the truth"—in each and every one of its sneaky incarnations—has lurked in stanzas all along. Because poets are still doing what we've been doing all along—serving as unerring and resolute witnesses, calling it like we see it, and lending lyricism and light to the chaos in an attempt to make the hardest of hard truths a little easier to stomach.

Of course, there's that nagging question: *What is truth anyway?* That query has always been the nagging stuff of nightmares and—lucky us—we writers are asked more frequently than anyone else.

I believe that truth in poetry is realizing the strength of our root, as Ukrainian poet Julia Kolchinsky does here in "On the 100th day of war in my birthplace:" from her spellbinding book *Parallax*:

in a country named outskirt, a city
named river, on a street named goddess
of the hunt, born in a government-assigned
apartment where our balcony was my preferred
place to sleep while my papa sang
inappropriate songs about alcoholics treating their dogs better
than their women & a neighborhood Baba
would shout up from the courtyard,

He's ruining the child with that language.

Now, I sing my children to sleep
in that same mother tongue [...]

Julia, one of this year's Miller Williams runners-up, came to this country as a Jewish refugee in the early 1990s. In her poems, she clutches at a feeling of home that is both unfamiliar and deeply treasured, longs for all that was left behind, struggles to come to terms with the rampant violence devastating a landscape that still, in so many encouraging and heartbreaking ways, belongs to her.

After reading Julia's manuscript, I could only sit with its cogency, reflecting upon its fierce lyric and how an oft-told story—that of the distant daughter of a country now embroiled in war—takes on singular force. These are poems of the unsettled moment, urgent and restless, deftly crafted to illustrate how war becomes part of the migrant's body, how its sole purpose is to change what truth truly is.

In John Allen Taylor's *To Let the Sun*, another of 2025's stellar runners-up, the truth is resolute and resounding. It troubles the poems the way a bomb troubles what dares to surround it.

There is no one who lives this life unbothered. We are all, in some way, wounded. If you are a conscious human of hurtin' age, it's a given that your heart is breaking as you read this. Loved ones die, fortunes are lost and made and lost again, reputations crumble, diseases slash lifelines. Our bodies are pummeled, ignored, taken for granted, invaded. We constantly strive to fold and carve and mold ourselves toward normal.

How?

Poets write our way into the lives we envision. But first we must write into and past the wounding.

That's so much of what John is doing in *To Let the Sun*. He does so without hiding in the squeaky folds of sentiment or resorting to the tired language that latches itself to trauma. In these captivating poems, there are regrets dissected, pain tugged to the surface, love celebrated, secrets searching for voice.

Here. The opening lines of John's heartrending "Golden Pothos":

> I refuse to imagine
> a changed past, another
> childhood. *What if he*
> *never touched you?* she asks
> & I shrug into my cowardice
> *I don't know, I do not know.*
> A pothos hangs over us
> where we sit on the bed.
> The vine doesn't know summer
> rages outside the window,
> doesn't fret about the next
> watering, doesn't remember
> falling from its perch
> on the drive from Boston
> to Detroit when we moved
> last July. It remembers
> the shears, after.

If you ended that passage with a sudden intake of breath, you're not alone. I too was spurred to experience the largeness of moment through the smallness of what the poet allowed me to see. In this poem, as in so many others in *To Let the Sun*, I heard the thick thread of once-suppressed pain woven throughout the now out-loud lines. I heard the wounding, and I was spellbound as John went about his necessary work. But these are not—as we hear all too often—"poems of healing." These memories bellow and screech instead of whisper.

Once I'd made my manuscript selections and learned John's name, I spent hours reading his forays into the minefield, his crafting of truths with their tangled beginnings in the mind of a child, now splendidly wrought in the hands of a poet whose dazzling and devastating poems are his root to the world.

As John declares in "Confession,"

> Only a razor in a steady hand
> could have left this mark.

If you ended that couplet with a sudden intake of breath, you're not alone.

When normal respiration resumes, read this snippet from "Alarm," an offering in Lena Moses-Schmitt's *True Mistakes*—the third of our runners-up (these are in no particular order, by the way).

> This morning, the sound of water rushing underground.
> I don't know what this means, or where the source.
> As if I'm walking on a paved-over river. Fossilized current,
> old patterns of thought. What am I grieving?
> A few blocks away, a truck backs up,
> releasing a slow series of beeps, endless
> ellipses, and I realize it's the same
> alarm that's been going off inside me,
> distant and silent, all year.

What *are* we grieving? The truths we're forced to confront are the thousand answers to that single question. Grieving is a constant. As I'm writing this, the television in the next room blares with news of another child wielding an assault weapon, another school haunted and slapped quiet, another four lives lost. Tomorrow we will reenter the world, warily meet each other's eyes, and nod imperceptibly, acknowledging our ritual of shared terror.

Lena is who we are when we're back in our rooms alone, pummeling the mirror with questions that leave scars. After all, the first truth must be always us—and *True Mistakes* is a lyrical surface for our vulnerabilities, an admission that the human family, for all its boisterous songs and bright colors, is a family of fracture.

The tender but forthright avowals in *True Mistakes* are ones I recognize and have struggled to hear. In these poems, Lena is in frank conversation with her flawed, confounded, and tentative self, and within that revelatory dialogue lurks a truth for every reader.

And now. [FANFARE]

When you happen upon an unforgettable manuscript written by someone you have never met, you instinctively begin to formulate a picture of the poet. You assume educational backdrop, ethnicity, hometown, time spent as a poet, political leanings, creative influences, family life, etc. You can't help it. You're often wrong, sometimes you're right. But you can't help it.

I pictured someone very much like Greg Rappleye, but—and this has nothing at all to do with physical bulk—I didn't picture quite as much of him as there actually is. Not even close.

That said, there's a lot that goes into being Greg Rappleye—winner of the 2000 Brittingham Prize in Poetry, revered teacher at Hope College in Michigan, a frequent presence in the savviest lit journals, and the artist behind the most impressive manuscript in this competition. (Yes, yes, I know—*arguably*. But what the judge says goes.) He's a solid, upright, immensely talented poet who (here comes the part that threw off my conjured portrait of said poet) just happens to write nerve, sonically explosive lines like—

> But above all our American nights, this was legend—
> screams, wingéd ashtrays, shattered bottles,
> a wall splattered with blood that would copper-brown
> as a martyr's relic, holy and untouched,
> into a new millennium, the Philco and its duct-taped
> bunny ears, chucked out the door to smithereens,
> the berserk words tumbling through spittle
> flecked lips and *Looney Tunes* lipstick,
> the syllables of which we knew
> were mortal sins the nuns would drag us off
> to confess were we to chant them, in sing-song
> voices, on the whirl-around at St. Mary's School,
> until Mam was locked in the bathroom
> slashing at air with a straight-edge,
> primed to cut Da's throat, and Da outside the door
> flailing with a spike maul, shattering fat-wood
> to smoker chips, and my sister, age 8,
> came whispering to our rooms.

Uh, wow.

Barley Child goes on and on that way, full to bursting with heat and motion and sound and rampaging narrative, rich with human triumph and frailty, populated with memorable characters whose lives waste no time entering our own. I read the entire manuscript out loud, reveling in the energized unreeling of narrative, the robust characters, but most of all, the unrelenting *song* of it all.

There's no way to read *Barley Child* and not wallow in the midst of all that aural audaciousness, no way not to live within its story, no way to close the book after that last line in that last poem and not believe all of it to be true. True in the way that a poet sees truth—as a resolution for anguish, as acknowledging home, as an unswerving bond between sound and story.

Judging this year's competition was insanely difficult. They've all been. Astounding poems are everywhere, and poets continue unearthing truths when we most need them. Thanks to my stalwart screeners, who passed along the very best, you now hold the best in your hands.

PATRICIA SMITH

INITIAL SINGULARITY

Neurodiverse sounds like universe but I can't write that world so I try a villanelle.

The world is cruel to most, just look:
the tire-tracked doe's severed neck,
my child's eyes when you realize

his difference. He won't stop
talking, touching, staring, hurting.
The world is cruel too. Most just look

and marvel, *He doesn't even seem*
autistic . . . So friendly . . . Speaks another tongue.
My child's eyes when your real lies

hit his ears. My hands and heart,
the pills and therapy, can't hold back
the world. It's cruel to most. Just look

at any roadkill. Have you stopped
long enough to see his open eyes?
The world is cruel to most, just look:

On the 100th day of war in my birthplace:

The rhododendrons keep blooming
despite the blood. I don't dream or touch

my husband. The toilet's
been collecting a black rim
at water level no matter how often

I scrub. My son refuses to sit until it's gone.
My hands smell like my great-grandmother's
last years in this country, though her childhood
in Bila Tserkva must have smelled similar, ammonia

mixed with goat milk & wheat before famine
took them, or lilac & spilled oil, when she'd steal
away to the city. Before war
took the city too. My children scream
as though they know

what's happening. I ask they use "inside voices"
in Russian. There's no direct translation—
home voice, *damashni golos'*, I say. My tongue
hurts my mouth. I don't eat or clean
my body. I claw at my scalp to find
unintended gifts my children

left behind—lime playdough, floss, an uneaten
french fry. Their bodies use mine
as treasure chest & waste bin.
I stopped listening to the news in the car
since "Breaking, active shooter inside
an elementary school" echoed on the way
to my son's psychiatrist appointment.

I blast '90s pop rock, "You're a god and I
am not and I just thought that you would know,"
recalling how my son asked why people go
to church when he saw 21 chairs with 21 sunflower
wreaths outside of one, *To pray to God*, I explained.
Why? God doesn't exist, he said. *Some people
believe and it helps them*, I clarified & he asked,
Do you? reminding me the chairs & wreaths

mean someone died or many someones. Dead,

he repeated, churches mean dead. *Sometimes,
I believe*, I said. *Other times*...

I spend $5.75 on a latte & count
the Ukrainian flags I pass on
Crouchwood, Longwood, Brentwood, Kenwood.

It's been weeks since my last donation & I've stopped counting
our dead. *Do you speak Russian?* my son asks
every stranger. *No? Why not? I do! My mom's from Ukraine.*
They always say how sorry they are

for my country as though they were the ones
at fault, & maybe, we are all to blame.
The checkout clerk at the Kroger has cotton
in her ears the way I was forced to as a child
on our transatlantic, immigrant flight, soaked

in eucalyptus or iodine to prevent
ear infections. Her name tag says Maryna,
& when she hears me speaking to my daughter,
A familiar language, she says, *I'm afraid to ask
where you're from.* She exhales relief, tells me
her mother is in an occupied territory,

It's been 85 days since we've spoken. She rings
up our ice cream & hopes
I'll come back. The vanilla melts
on the way home & the children throw fits & want
more sprinkles, longing for solid to stay
solid. Sitting on the closed toilet lid, hiding
from their screaming, I am still born

in a country named outskirt, a city
named river, on a street named goddess
of the hunt, born in a government-assigned
apartment where our balcony was my preferred

place to sleep while my papa sang
inappropriate songs about alcoholics treating their dogs better
than their women & a neighborhood Baba
would shout up from the courtyard,

He's ruining the child with that language.

Now, I sing my children to sleep
in that same mother tongue, in their American-

born beds. I hear my son's echo,
If I can't see it, it doesn't exist. I tuck them in
& pray, wordless. *You're my sunflower,* my son whispers

in English, tugging at my hair
like petals & wishing *don't die, don't die,*
even if he doesn't believe, *don't die,*
he reaches, not for god,

but whatever language
is closest to Mama.

I.

CARBON

Carbon, in fact, is a singular element: it is the only element that can bind itself in long stable chains without great expense of energy, and for life on earth (the only one we know so far) precisely long chains are required. Therefore carbon is the key element of living substance.

—PRIMO LEVI

I do not mention the war to my six-year-old son but somehow his body knows.

My face in his hands
before bed, he asks, *if I cut you*
in half, will you be even?
I am silent. Expecting
mothers in Mariupol are cut
by invisible hands. Children
cut off from water. *Because you have*
two eyes + two ears + two cheeks
+ so much hair + your mouth
can have two halves
so you would be even, right?
He wants simple math.
Breath that outlasts
violence. *You ÷ 2 =*
2 even you's. He isn't asking
anymore. He is making me
monument. *You would still be*
if I cut you in half. Small hands
demand a splitting. *If you*
cut me in half, I tell him,
I'd be dead.

Why write another poem about the moon

with all her names & animals
dragged out into the March sky

eagle moon goose moon crow-comes-
back moon because what my mother

moon drags out of her mouth is less
animal because she doesn't know

to blame the sky for my son's phases
his "bad behavior" or his father's

"sick genes" passed down by blood
& breath & blood on the moon

means death & *if he's this bad now*—
the broken glass & bruises & bites,

the time he pushed his sister down
a flight of stairs—*what will the future hold*

she says afraid of what his hands
will do *you must discipline it out of him*

or else like moon always returning
to her fullness he too will turn

into his father & I will love them both
& foolishly protest the cycle *there are worse things*

he could turn into I say & she asks *what?*
refuses to read the link to signs & symptoms

of ADHD & autism spectrum disorders & googles
"boarding schools for bad boys" while I turn

to his hands & the worm moon & all the earthworms
she drags out like the one on my mother's front step

held more gentle than breath in my son's palm
as he begged to bring it inside to keep & love

to hold this way forever but my mother
wouldn't have it in her house

so we left it there on stone & the next day
look it left its skin behind for me my son said

a gift & I just couldn't bring myself
to tell him this leaving is what death

can look like so under that same moon
renamed sugar moon strong wind moon

sore eye moon mother always mother
moon I nodded *yes a gift*

Watching Masha i Medved as Russia Invades Ukraine

Mishka, nu Mishka, blares in Russian
through one ear as CNN coverage

of the first-day missiles falling
on my birthplace echoes through

a blue earbud in the other. My children
are on the couch drinking their morning

milk and stuffing their mouths full
of warm croissants, watching a blond Slavic girl

wrap a giant bear around her finger. *Mishka*,
she tenderly calls, little bear, and he

reluctantly does whatever is asked—prepares
elaborate meals of kashas with dried fruits

and homemade cherry-currant-gooseberry
preserves and stroganoff and stews and

smoked fish with five kinds of potatoes, and
if she but whispers in her small,

high-pitched voice, *Mishka*, he will carry her
and a menagerie of animals, in his big-bear arms,

across a swamp and field of sunflowers,
to safety. More missiles fall on Kyiv.

The airport in the city I was born
is bombed. I don't remember it.

My Dnipro. The home where I collected
chestnuts by the Dnieper River or ate

small spheres of ice cream from a shop
called Pinguin or held my mother's hand

when the streets flooded, and she lifted me up
to walk the rim of rusted fountains. *Incoming call*

from Dom, meaning *Home*, interrupts the news.
Mama tells me she finally reached her childhood

friend. They spoke as shells fell and maybe
Marina could see fires through her window.

My mother never thought this would happen.
None of us did. The subway stations turned

bomb shelters the way they were in the war
her parents lived through and grandparents

died fighting. *Not while there are still those alive*
*to remem*ber, she said. *How could he do this*

while they are still alive? she repeats
to her mother over tea and tears

and disbelief. *They thought they'd never have to endure it again.* Ice falls

in Arkansas, and my children demand another snack and episode of *Masha*

in their mother's tongue, my mother-tongue. This mouthful of history

we chew and chew until it chokes us.

Dear Fellow Ukrainian Poet-Mama,

The tomatoes have gone bad
in the bottom drawer and there
are tornado warnings—I thought
you'd like to know about my fridge.
When my son asked for a scary story,
I thought of all the frozen fruit
that will not rot, so I told him, when I was
his age on the Black Sea, I stuck my finger
into a beached log and a wasp chased me
down the Odesa sand and my hand
swelled to a sun and it's raining so hard here,
like what I imagine our grandfather's
combat boots sounded like leaving,
and there, my mother put a halved tomato
on the sting because acid
was the only thing we had
to stop swell, and here, the baby
just woke wailing and our street
is flooding and I try to shut her mouth
with my breast so her brother stays
asleep as she wants and wants and not
what I can give and I think, I have no ark
but this ragged body that never learned
to float. Still, she clings to its faults, its flaws
and fallacies, unaware of all the ways
its failing us. She doesn't mind
the tomatoes, how our past
keeps filling our children's mouths.
How do they not notice it's gone

so very bad? The day after
Easter Sunday, nothing's risen but
fog, and a week after Passover,
bread and the Red Sea stay
unleavened in our people's homes.
Little did either testament
know flood and sickness
were just the beginning. My son acts out
the plagues, becoming beast, lice, frog,
and locusts, slamming his hands and trains
on hardwood like boots and trains and this
rain and the men he comes from
who never came home. He throws
heavy things at his sister, unafraid
of death or hurt because what child
of any history understands
permanence. *Parents always
come back*, they tell him in school.
How do you explain this
to your children? Our air
turned plague? Street
turned river? Present turned
strange past even our parents
couldn't have imagined. I wish I had
your gift for jokes and baking,
for beginning in laughter, so instead,
I'll try to end there, with my children,
their bellies so full these days, faces
the opposite of famine, laughing

harder than this rain, I swear,
laughing like there are no endings.
I guess that's the punchline
after all, *I'm going to eat you
like a tomato*, my son says
into his sister's rising stomach
and their laughter, so hard
and full, it wakes the dead.

The Past Doesn't Rise Like Smoke

I don't envy even
      a second of your life,
my mother says, *not*
      a single second. Babushka
agrees, pities me, the two
      unmanageable kids,
the disabled husband.
      It's just so hard for you,
she says, recalling
      how her face burned
when she was left
      on the top bunk of the train
evacuating her family
      from Kyiv, the city not yet
surrounded, but certain
      to fall. War, more than
memory. War
      the way she names
her life. Missing
      without a trace. Her father
stayed back, died, and after him,
      she named her daughter
Light. *He has to lie at Babyn Yar.*
      Where else? she asks, watching
the third-night candle smoke.
      I do not say black earth
is made of all our dead.
      I do not say I'm tired
of counting them. I say,

I will keep trying
to find his name.
        I say, our people
are made of miracle
        and half believe it
when I ask my father
        about his dead.
He doesn't know
        their names,
just that they never left
        Odesa. The *shochet*
neighbor survived, he recalls,
        severed chicken heads
the godly way and lit
        Hanukkah candles
in their courtyard. He remembers
        smoke rising
against December,
        gray on black until
there was no trace
        of flame. But the past
doesn't rise like smoke.
        There is nowhere for it to go
missing. The past is every
        fried potato and charred wick.
My son's nail singed, singing
        over the candles,
the wrong words
        of a Hebrew blessing

we were never taught.
       The past rises
like swifts, perhaps, who stay
          aerial for months, digging
for earth in the clouds,
          abandoning the sky only
to make more birds,
          who will rise and rise
in swarms from narrow
          chimneys, who will refuse
to smoke, who will return only
          once having left
their names carved
          in unsuspecting air.

Omen

We heard it in the wall first,
      the morning scurrying
            behind our headboard,
     rats, we thought, and blamed
the neighbors. A few sharp fists

and all would quiet. How wings
      can sound like feet. Bird
          like what it preys on.
     Let me out
no different from

let me in. No telling how
     its iridescent neck like oil-spill
         ended up perched on our
     bathroom door. Raven?
Wren? Starling? Perhaps

a common grackle. A bird
     in the house means
         message at best, means
     death within these walls,
means there are still walls

and a house to hold them.
     A dead bird or white bird
        is worse. My son called ours
     house bird, begged, *please,*
don't leave. It didn't listen.

Black wings to the fridge
      then out the back into sunlight.
            A bird in the house means
      house bird. Means my son
will keep looking every time

he goes outside, *maybe, it'll find*
      my worm, he says, *and they can be*
            friends. How love can sound
      like what it devours. Bird
like the boy it preys on.

Bird the closest prayer gets
      to god. A bird in the house
            means death. A bird in the wall
      means broken. A bird means,
please, don't leave.

The Ukrainian Flag Stares through the Balsam Fir from Larry's Farms

Just take it he said & I doubted
generosity *are you sure?* still $30 short
I've learned nothing is free
in this country his
white mustache curled
to a smile *I'm Larry & this*
is the South & these are my trees
how easy to claim what soil gives
to own trees & bodies
to give them away to strangers
so my children can hang
the shatterproof ornaments & ask for more
light while in Ukraine
the bulbs won't spark & heat won't radiate
the soil will stay
snow-covered & theirs &
in my house strings & strings
of electric rainbow dazzle
trail the evergreen & walls & wind
my children's small limbs
here it's barely cold enough
to light a fire but we can & do
with oak & crabapple we home
its added glow so everything
smells of invited smoke & pine
not invaded smoking sky where
the windows flicker with candlelight
& shellings & tomorrow
I will bake gingerbread & fry

latkes & light the candles
forbidden in my Soviet childhood
tomorrow I will pray
to a god I don't believe in
for more miracle tomorrow
I will still have been born
from darkness & wick & tonight
when I lift my daughter
to place the silver star on the highest branch
& my American mother-
in-law takes a photo
the only light will be the yellow-
blue horizon of the flag
frozen in the window behind us

10 Months Since the Full-Scale Invasion as Math Problem

10 months = 305 days =
incalculable = my son is great
at math > decent at speaking
the tongue of the invader + at 7
he can add double digits in his head
can even do some basic × and ÷
> he's afraid of the windows
in his room = they don't add up =
they can always shatter = someone
can always come in < they could be carrying
an ax or scythe ≠ I tell him they won't =
something inside of him is terrified
anyways = some part of him knows
he comes from a bloodied land
of missing bodies = knows his body
is closer to the dead than the living + he
doesn't want to die + the dead live
in the letters of his name + no matter
how high he can count in days + years
numbers won't lead to certainty =
each night he tells me, *I must sleep in the dark*
= *that's horrible* = the proximity to =
the possibility of not waking
doesn't come out
of his mouth =
night always comes.

Why write another poem about the moon?

From earth, your thumb, little
sun, is large enough
to cover her whole face.

Because comfort is someone
staring at that same
celestial body. Parallax fixes

little—its geometry
of eyes—but holds us
accountable to distance.

Because stone becomes
brightest light pleading
for more of itself.

Our hands for more
of another's. Because you
told me, *we are all made*

of stars & I didn't believe.
So you turned comet
through the house, a cloud

of vapor in your wake—
electrons and ions
born in the belly of stars.

You held my body in your small
hands—careful now—whispering
stardust stardust. How skin

holds bone as though it were
the sky, our insides
constellations refusing

eternal shape. You taught me
to believe we all hold fragments
of first light.

II.

HYDROGEN

I experienced retrospective fear and at the same time a kind of foolish pride, at having confirmed a hypothesis and having unleashed a force of nature. It was indeed hydrogen, therefore: the same element that burns in the sun and stars, and from whose condensation the universes are formed in eternal silence.

—PRIMO LEVI

On Raising Mountains

Mama, can I
kiss you? he asks,
already reaching
for whatever part of me
is closest, easiest
to grab. His toddler hands
already mountains. His fingers
rain. You can track
the distance of a storm
counting the seconds
between thunder and light.
You can smell it
long before.
How to teach him
asking
is not enough?
Mama, kiss me,
he demands, *hard,*
wants me to press
into each of his palms.
Their cherry pits. My lips
around his bones. Wants
to do the same to mine.
My hands a flooded
river. An orchard. My hands
not mine. *Eat me,* he says,
I'm a cookie, and means
sweetness, his fingers
and belly, means:

I just want love
I do not have
a language for.
His hands already
squeezing tight
my cheeks. My face
between two mountains.
How to teach him
what consent
should feel like?
The seconds between
thunder and light.
A downpour. Hard,
I kiss each
of his knuckles.

Why write another poem about the moon

when my son is surrounded
by the severed heads
of Barbies I spent

a decade loving
but haven't touched
for three of his lifetimes?

how long after he ran
his fingertips so gently
across their hair

did he tear the plastic
skulls from their torso trunks
and leave them naked

like birch branches
from my childhood stripped
of bark by summer thunderstorm

and strewn so far
who knows what tree
they once belonged to?

the doll I carried
across the Atlantic
is hit the worst.

her pelvis cracked
in half and head
missing altogether

its mess of dirty curl
just like his own and eyes
too much like mine. *Moons*

he says *they look*
like hairy moons
my son their sun and I

am terrified
for every woman
every moon he longs to touch

It's not the dark

that scared me
but how faces change
in the absence of light.

Each toy becoming
animal & every animal
more human, more

fear. My mother
hadn't stopped breathing
in her sleep yet, father

hadn't taken up insomnia
& I would dim the lights enough
to see the dolls' eyes safely tucked

back in their skulls. *Never sleep
with your closet open,*
my mother insisted, *Who knows*

what could come out.
So I grew up afraid of everything
behind closed doors

or lids, closed lips especially, afraid
to open mine.
I'd swallowed far too many

lightning bugs, wings
against my larynx, trachea
        on fire. Secretly, I liked the ache

        between suffocation
& flight—afraid to let the dark out.
        At night, I dreamed our history.

Shadows cling to the walls.
        My son makes his fingers
harmless, beak or prey—

        duck-bill, bunny ears—he lingers
in bedtime stories, fears
        little & reaches

where he cannot see.
        My mother would have taught him
fear by now—closets & strangers.

        Instead, I let him hug them, knowing
caution will be easier to teach
        than love. I give him

shadows, a book
        of insect & manmade wings
we project onto the ceiling

with a flashlight. But if I open
my mouth against the past,
        swallowed fireflies would light

these pages. They survive
        in jars for days, so why not years
inside a fearful body? My son's

        face would turn
all wonder & aerial.
        His mouth, a lid, hands

open to catch the swarm,
        to swallow & return them,
wingless, back into his dark.

Cataloguing Home, Dnipro to Little Rock

Guitar ballads with the lights   off
power gone   many nights
horses know how to swim   but not far
not well   Mama says   it happened
only once   how memory
doubles back   on itself
a song about a sinking ship   a thousand
horses below deck   the juice box
with a bendy straw   raw hot dogs
from the street vendor   who only spoke
Ukrainian   his gray barrette   the river
always   the river   and the city
along the river   still standing   her chestnuts
& lilac   so heavy   they drown
in water   *people climbed into lifeboats*
clung to boards   the horses swam alongside
like a floating amber island   the preschool teacher
who threw   wet rags at my face
when I wouldn't stop   talking
the cots creaking at naptime   boards creaked
under hooves too   soup scalding my tongue
my tongue   won't stop
making language   the wrong
language now   perhaps Russian
has always been   wrong
but it is   my mother's   & mine   &
the ship was named *Gloria* & when I speak
to my children   when I sing

power out   again   no tornadoes
in Ukraine   just rain & rain   floods
spread everywhere   but here
far from home   inside my house
in Arkansas   how south & deep
my tongue has gone   mothering
after the tornado   my children's
beds creak too   my street   a river
at first it was easy to swim   the horses
thought the ocean   a river
this city   a graveyard   of torn tree
limbs   the power stays
gone for days   the oak & honey locust
almost touch the house   almost
my husband saws the smaller branches
down to candle holders   flame
gets close enough to touch the bark
almost   the whole house
smells of smoke & almost gone
I can almost taste   home   almost
how I pity them   how they never saw land
the gas stove   in Ukraine
lit while I pruned & reddened
in the tub   for hours   water added
from a tea kettle   eucalyptus & withering
windows fogged   heavy
boiled water   poured over   toddler flesh
my children   can spend hours

38

in the bath   soaking & softening   peeling
like new   potatoes   water
the body that separates & binds us
how they never saw land   our homes
unsung   unsinking   water
the only quiet   home

When my son says, *I don't love you*, I want to tell him about lilacs

how sometimes   I don't love them
their careless smell   of childhood   & sudden
bloom   their sweetness lingering to rot
& sometimes   I don't love   his grandmother   who always
loves lilacs   & smells of them   when making threats
of suicide   if I marry the man   who will become
his father & all   the lilacs   in her garden
will die   if I move away   or say
the words   I don't
& sometimes   I don't love
coffee   if it's gone warm
or the bed   when I am too far
from hitting it   or the pillow
sometimes   I fucking hate
the pillow   when I bite it
when making love   isn't
actually loving & I won't say
fuck   in front of my son
no matter how much I want to
I won't tell him   that sometimes
I don't love   his mouth   & hands
biting   & scratching
his head of curls   drilling
into my stomach   or
slamming   into the wall   & sometimes
I want to tell him   all the things
I do not love   but instead
I reassure him   after each *I don't love you,*
Mama, how much   *I do I do*

I don't know how to   love
without him
how the lilacs will keep
coming   year after year
how rot   is its own sweetness

Am I a bad mother:

if when I stepped on a lightning bug & dragged its luminescence
across our front step, I thought
about my children?

if its neon light traced the shape of a child's finger
streaking shower glass?

if while on the carpet—needles climbing up my tailbone from sitting
too long as the children fight sleep—I am still thinking about the crunch
of thorax?

if exoskeleton sounds too much like human bone? a throat
breaking? a heart? a baby sparrow's fall from its nest
snapped hollow?

if I imagine wings, daggers, teeth?

if flight & fall have everything in common?

if firefly is closer to the truth & flame, like fall, is also flight?

if I tell you the bug or fly (does name matter
without fire or light?) was almost dead
when I found it, blinking silent
morse code & I wished my children could have seen
its final shine?

if I craved to be the thing underfoot all along, ribcage
cracked, heart exposed & glowing, glowing, even more
beautiful now that I am gone?

Hurricane

One hand cinched
    around my throat,
        my son reaches
    his pointer finger
through my trachea,
    morning breath
        sucked clean.
    I cough & cough—
how much of me
    he takes, how hard
        his squeeze & puncture?
    Not strong
enough to open
    a gallon of milk,
        but enough hard
    to hurt. He asks about pain,
already certain of it
    & old enough
        to mean as much
    as rain means
to flood.
    His touch
        unasked for
    gift. Consent
a thing I teach & teach
    but cannot show.
        Torrential rain
    another name for us
both trying to come up for air.

He brushes
        my neck with fingertips,
You can't touch
anyone this way, I say,
        & he keeps stroking,
                gentle, insistent, letting
        fingers fall like water
into the dip where skin
        is thinnest, where
                he can feel
        air fill & lift the body.
Hours later, I still
        don't know
                how to reclaim
        this air as mine.
We have a tea party
        of black & herbal, double
                bergamot & lemon
        ginger, acid & dried
flowers tear
        my throat. My neck
                the gill of every fish
        who's known
a hook. Each swallow,
        a tinge, a barb,
                a child's bone lodged
        inside my windpipe,
but baby boy,
        you have always been
                uncontainable wind.

Hail

Our summer ground is covered
        in fallen cherry blossoms, melting
                because they were never
        petals. I listen to thunder and look up
meaning again, because so little
        makes sense—fires, floods,
                wars upon wars—origins
        rarely help. Still, I search. Still, hail
means health, prosperity, and good
        luck first. It means cheers. Hail drinking
to forget or remember. Hail my children,
        their full bellies and hearts. Their persistent,
                hungry mouths. Hail
        means kind hello as much
as falling ice. At first, it sounded like my son
        slamming action figures into the walls,
                so I didn't notice, and the smell
        of my unwashed hair after too many
chlorinated swims, taste of lavender, medicinal,
        bitter, on my children's cheeks, lather
                never thoroughly rinsed
        from their curls. My son's afraid,
so we tell him the sky
        is hungry, clouds grumble
                like his stomach.
        He doesn't believe this.
Knows nature is
        not body. Asks, how much it hurt
                when he pushed his sister
        off the loft and she hailed down,

her ulna snapping like shattered
　　ice, bending the radius
　　　　to the arch of the rainbow after.
　　He asks, if he goes out
and lets the hail hit him now, will it hurt
　　that much? I do not answer.
　　　　　The secret of silence
　　is not that we keep things
from our children, but that we have
　　so few answers ourselves. When split
　　　　in half, a hailstone shows rings
　　like a tree or onion, the original
ice at the center, then layers
　　of encasing growth crystals.
　　　　　Each from a different hungry cloud,
　　a different height in the atmosphere.
Each line, a border between places
　　we will never know or touch.
　　　　　What borders are there
　　between bodies? Between us
and our children? My son longs
　　to hold a frozen rock, to crush it
　　　　or perhaps just feel it
　　melt against his palm. Hail
his longing. We watch the pellets fall,
　　his forehead pressed
　　　　to fiberglass. I keep
　　the door closed. Keep him
close, inside.

What does the vulture say to the snowman(?) or how my son is learning to tell jokes(.)

He is trying to wrap
his mind, like a blanket,
around humor. *Knock Knock!*
You have to say: Who's there?
He instructs if answer
isn't immediate. *Orange.* Orange
who? *Orange.* Orange who?
Orange you glad I didn't say . . . wait
it was Banana! Let's do it again.
And again. And again. He will
repeat until he gets his version
of right. *Get it?* He will ask
laughing, mouth crow-open
and bellyful shaking, sometimes
falling on the floor, other times
just falling. He won't notice
whether you laugh in response.
What did the chocolate chip
say to the pancake? Even if
you aren't listening. *You're brown,*
get it? Because they're both
brown. At the evaluation
they said, *He overexaggerates*
expressions, exclaims, and repeats
things he doesn't understand.
You hadn't noticed.
That's just his way
of telling jokes you thought. *Dead.*
Dead. Dead. His teacher asks you
to make it stop. *Our cat*

is dead. Grandpa is dead. Great-
grandpa and Great-grandma
dead. Dead. Dead. Dead.
He's making others
cry. *He scares them*, she writes,
and tells you he enjoys it.
He just wants
a reaction, you try
to explain, *What did the caterpillar say*
to the butterfly? You've changed.
You want to show her he's reaching
for humor. You want
to remind her of the seven
purple butterflies he drew
after she told him
they remind her of her dead
mother. Told him seeing
wings made her happy.
You haven't moved
in hours, said the vulture, guess
I can eat you. Get it, Mama?
Because vultures eat dead things
and a snowman isn't dead.
The way "dead" fits
in his mouth
like a punchline.

III.

PHOSPHOROUS

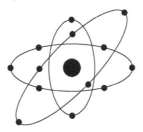

Phosphorus has a very beautiful name (it means "bringer of light"), it is phosphorescent, it's in the brain, it's also in fish, and therefore eating fish makes you intelligent; without phosphorus plants do not grow . . . it is in the tips of matches, and girls driven desperate by love ate them to commit suicide; it is in will-o'-the-wisps, putrid flames fleeing before the wayfarer.

—PRIMO LEVI

Summer Camp Can't Fit the Shape of Flame

"We cannot accommodate
the needs of your child"
                        means find another place
            for him to be

himself & scorch like   in the story
            the cat's house burns down

            & no animal will let her in because   there is no room
                        for her for him

                                                    inside

            & the fire won't die & "I'm sorry
                        I wish we could

do more" means there is nothing
            they will do &   sobs & sobs

                        & can't   stop
            because *I just want to go back*

            to see my friends means
                        he thought for the briefest moment

            he had friends & the lake
held his body

            tight enough & the sun
                        was only reflection

                    not blister & the ticks
          didn't bite his ankles & even

      if they did *it's okay*
he says & promises to
                                                    try harder
                          & be better &
                                                    keep all that him

          inside & "I know what you are

                going through"
          means they have no idea & *it's not*

      your fault I keep repeating as he sobs
                & asks to be rocked like a   baby

with all the heft of a grown   boy & limbs
          flail like young branches until

          he laughs & forgets
tomorrow & summer is long

                          & hot & lingers   everywhere
          his body touches & accommodate

means "to make fit"
          but he doesn't

fit the shape they've named
    child & needs them

                                       to change

their shape & "we cannot"

                                       means

did they even

                                       try

Violet Is Another Name for Touch

Perhaps he didn't know his body
        was already weapon
                and so became the hurt—

the force that leaves its mark
        pressed deep into another.
                Perhaps he wanted nothing

        more than touch.

We depend on violent
        prepositions, perhaps on just
                the violence. In the lunch line,

he held a small boy's
        finger, tenderly

                at first, then pushed it back

until, *I was waiting for him*

to cry, he admits, drilling
        his head into my stomach,
                the sun a bruise against the bones

        of oaks. *I didn't want to hurt*

him. The small boy's tears and face
        contorted to a soundless
                shriek is easy to name

ache—an unreachable

color outside my son's body. Violet
        perhaps or wholly
                violence. We name

the place another's shape begins

to purple. My son's hair
        catches in the zipper of my jeans
                —he doesn't recognize

his body's endings—its metal
        teeth full of curl. He doesn't
                yell, just pulls

        harder. *I'd rather hurt*

myself, he says. The only way
        his body knows to love
                another. And after,

he punches my arm and pinches
        his sister's, grabs her
                cotton candy cheeks.

Waiting for us

to plum, to pit, to turn crushed
     blueberry, he sobs, eyes
          swelling shut—nastic

flower heads. Touch
     a weighted
          blanket, a mouth, a hurt,

     sweet perennial—longing

deep as beetroot—
     we cannot keep it
          trapped inside.

How many poems can I write about my son's insatiable longing?

for a body / anyone's but his own / he counts
the minutes to any destination / grasps
flesh / skin / muscle / bone / his stuffed
red panda / wrings its neck / watches
it snap back in place / whispers
/ *I'm sorry* / does it again /again
with my neck / he is gentle now / massages
around the trachea / kneads the upper trapezius /
asks how firm / how fast / how deep
to sink his fingers / such care took years / my body
a scarred and patient teacher / he's still learning
tenderness / strangers' bodies are more
permissive ground / mine / a minefield / *your heart
is so warm* / he says / *I wish I could reach in
and touch it* / a longing so innocent
he doesn't remember / the times he's tried /
failed / tried again / my heart still hot
against his palm / nail / canine / *you're a volcano*
/ he says / mouth hot against my neck /
just kidding / there's no laughter / *I know
I am* / dormant / smoke rising / soaking
my hair / that campfire scent
/ so longed for / until
it won't wash out

When a friend texted to say her son's fish died & the child won't stop wailing

I told her if my son had a single wish
he confesses would bring our cat

back from the dead though he was only
a year old when I found Ele P. Hant

motionless in his litter box
even in death the cat named elephant

was the most respectable animal
refusing to sleep in my bed for a whole week

the way he had for eleven years & my one-year-old
spent most of his life pulling & smacking & chasing

the cat with hands the opposite of what we think
is love but what does a child see as tenderness? none of us

remain children long enough to know & I asked
how long they'd had the fish? more than a year she said pandemic

pet meant to help her son through absence & if not
replace grandparents & playmates at least give him someone

to watch through water & it must have helped
teach him how we can love without

touch & this morning I write to see
how they are doing her son was inconsolable

she's worried what this means for bigger
human losses & I said my son is only afraid

of two things: getting a shot & losing me
all other pain abstraction I say our people

make every loss catastrophe & every death
all death & Isaac Bashevis Singer wrote we are all walking

cemeteries carrying our dead inside us
but she writes there has been no mention

of the fish or its death & kids are resilient I say we
are resilient I say resilience & every time

the word distances from its origin "an act
of rebounding" jumping back resilience

meaning not survival but our ability to exist
that much more distant from one another

Since becoming my son's only friend, I've had to become Baba Yaga.

He wants to get boiled alive in my cauldron.
To be eaten whole. *Don't spit out my bones,* he says.
He wants to burrow his mane of curls back
into my belly and beat me with sticks and pull
out my hair and sleep his face earthward
into my face. He wants to drown inside me.
Wants consumption. To be consumed.
Be all-consuming. He doesn't need
a mortar and pestle to fly. My body will always
do. Become everything and everyone
he makes believe. Become the hut on chicken's feet
and my mother, *baba,* grandma, old hag, babulya,
beloved. *Baba Yaga,* he says, *be my friend,*
because what lonely boy wouldn't fall in love
with the ugly he knows will swallow him?

Ferris Wheel

My children stare over the water, their lips
stretched, shining taffy over faces greased

in sunscreen and sticky soft serve, such smiles
only come when leaving ground with certainty

of return. Like cardinals or this state's northern
mockingbird, its apple blossom and pine. *Arkansas,*

I tell them the river's name and ask they say
goodbye. We count the revolutions, rises, the sun's

reaching for us through the white suspensions
of Memorial Bridge. We are moving across

the country, again. They are old enough
to remember the last time, to miss the city

we left. In Russian, this ride is called the devil's
wheel, not named after its inventor, but the inescapable

turning, trying, tiring lift, the desire to leave,
doomed or destined to come back. When I left

Ukraine, I was allowed to take one doll—the rest,
as little as it was, I abandoned. My children are packing

everything, stuffed horses and bears and fish
they haven't touched in years, board books

they've outgrown, torn blankets, softer
for the wear, puzzles with missing pieces, broken

crayons and dried-up markers. I try to throw away
the stick figures they drew, their earliest scribbles,

but end up cataloging every handprint turned
turkey or flower. My mother has a photocopy

of my Soviet passport and a pocket-notebook
marking my first-year's milestone. My art and toys begin

at six, when I am renamed something Americans
can pronounce. At four and seven, my children

may not remember this short-lived home
in the sweltering South, the tornado

that ripped through the oaks in our backyard, or
the ice storm that split the crabapple out front

the day bombs began to fall on their mother's
birthplace. They may forget the cat

buried behind the fence, the cairns they constructed,
stacking stones with small hands, quartz and basalt

and their shed skin. They may forget our dog,
older than both their years combined, who died

calm and quick, in front of the fireplace
while they were at school. They will certainly

forget her. The Ferris Wheel stops, and we are held
at the top. The moment is too long.

My older child says he is afraid, what if
we are stuck? what if we can't come back?

I assure him, we will, that turn fits inside
return and the ground is certain. I've left

enough times to know. Before the invasion,
I was planning a trip back to ride the devil's wheel

on the Dnieper River's shore. I hold my children
as we lower down and they glee how this

was the best ride of their lives, how they touched
the sky and saw the whole city and said

goodbye, how they want to return, to keep
and keep on turning. But we are out

of tickets, it's getting late, time to go
home, home, I say, but do not tell them

I am afraid too.

Why write another poem about the moon?

Mercury has two days left
in retrograde and the Mars
        rover just landed on sands

less red than imagined and my son
        drags my daughter
around the house

        in an oversized box convinced
he is wielding an interplanetary
        time-machine and he slams

the box flap on top of her
        and means to do it
and time keeps going her lip

        split red the shade I expected
him to turn her mouth
        without intention and I've raised

my voice I've screamed violet
        too many times and turned
redder than I ever imagined

        motherhood and when
nothing else worked his father snapped
        a leg off a Spiderman

action figure and threw it
     in the recycling bin and my son
wailed red and burning

     refusing to believe it couldn't be
fixed or time couldn't move
     back just this once or

my arms could refuse
     to hold him but we explained
calm and colorless

     some things once severed
can't be put back together
     some things like the moon

have to stay broken

IV.
OXYGEN

Among the various exploits, vital or destructive, which oxygen can perform, we varnish makers are interested above all in its capacity to react with certain small molecules such as those of certain oils, and of creating links between them, transforming them into a compact and therefore solid network.

—PRIMO LEVI

One Year Later

It's easy to look away from war
when your wallet's empty and sink is full,
when the land and people aren't yours,

when your children scream for more
of you, when your body's pulled
it's easy to look away from war.

The soil across the water to earth's core
brims blood, but look, the sunflowers still bloom
when the land and people aren't yours.

So, you focus on the daily chores,
dig out a trench of laundry—linens, wools—
it's easy to look away from war

with the dog barking, mailman at the door.
Your children speak a stranger's tongue at school,
the land and people aren't yours.

How does a house become a shore
no news can reach? Are we that cruel?
Or is it just that easy to look away from war
when the land and people aren't yours?

Tell me it gets easier

every new parent asks,
It doesn't, I say bluntly & something
        inside us shatters a little, not
hope, too large, uncontainable
        in the body, like sky or the layers
of ocean my son knows
        are named sunlight,
twilight, midnight, abyss, & trenches,
        the further down
the closer to war. *Tell me*
        it gets easier, they ask
to hear difficulty or darkness
        are temporary, but the depths
are endless not because
        they do not end but because
we've never reached the bottom.
        In water, the difference
between float / sink / swim / drown
        are matters of breath & motion,
little to do with light & everything
        with ease.
Endurance a resistance all its own.
        It doesn't, I say again, my face
reflected in the shallow sink
        that just won't drain.
It never gets easier, I exhale.
        We just grow used to bearing
difficulty. We hold our breaths
        long enough
to reach the surface.

Why write another poem about the moon

when every streak of white
rippled by metal-winged machine

my son names comet not plane
and reading about monarch butterflies

he wishes for wings
like anyone who's ever looked up

because the sky is only torn
in daylight and the sky

is every little boy trying
to hold his flight inside

and I tell him these trails
are clouds not comet tails

but just last night a meteor
exploded over the horizon

two states north and he wants
to see it and hear the body-rattling

boom the sky ripped out
of darkness by something strong enough

to stone and shine because
what is every little boy

if not speeding oxygen and iron
fractaled flame turned solid enough

to name and tear the sky
because my little boy once asked me

for the moon and learned
how much I cannot give him

After the third snow day in a row, I'm ready to throw the towel

into the fire   out the window
at the cardinal   clinging   to the broken
branch   limp   like a dislocated finger
at my feet   slippered & sore   from keeping
up   at my children   yes   their screaming
at my children   their faces   needing
always needing   more
pink paper & play   more water   more
food   different   from whatever I've made   more
more mama   closer than sound lets on   mama
from every room   echoes the house   & where
is she   where?   this me   named need
hiding under a sodden towel   ice thick
soaks frost & bitten toes   thick the body
they made of me   the towel   too wide to noose
the towel too   heavy to throw   fire
just embers now   barely a flash of red
through ash   too weak to thaw   barely the cardinal
picks at my mended bones   beak tender
relentless   my children
run feathered & flamed   tongues stretched
for falling shards   the sky lets herself throw
relentless   the towel
isn't big enough   to cover all of us
mama more more   mama
my children's need   relentless
& when in flight   the attendants warn
put on your oxygen mask first   before

assisting others   how to let the body
listen   when my children
inhale deep   relentless
my children   the only sky I know

I bring poets from Lviv, Ukraine, to my college class in Arkansas

through the computer screen   a loud   bang   a bomb   a fist perhaps
a body   broken   breaking *don't worry*   *it's okay*
the poet says   her partner shoves   a cat   into the virtual box
alongside them   the furry predator must   have knocked down
books   or worse

                        must have followed   its nature   to move
about the room   as though   all of it   were his   *we are safe*
the poet says in English   in Ukrainian her partner   clarifies
в Україні безпечного місця немає   in Ukraine no place is safe
in Ukraine   no place is   in Ukraine no place   in Ukraine   no
I speak a tongue   of violence   in Ukraine

                                    the poets move
between Slavics   *mova & rech'*   speech & speech   motion & river
he kisses her   barely bare shoulder   wipes a smudge   of lipstick
from the curve of chin   "why   is it important   to write   still
during war?"   my students   mouth   towards empathy
because people continue the poets say   *doing what they always do*   in hybrid
language   *in the same*   *places*

                                    I recall weeks
after the first shelling   Kyiv's sky   a charcoal canvas   I imagine nothing
like this American   south's cerulean March blue   when older kids
approached   my six-year-old   on the wire rope sling   spider
climbing tower   "What language   are you speaking?"
he is honest   *We speak*

            Russian   the elementary-school playground
hushes   the older kids   now louder   closer "You're Russians!?"
they climb   the steel-steady rungs   louder   closer
My mom's from Ukraine   from below I watch   white clouds wisp
his hair   maybe smoke   from my birthplace   reaching for us

even here "Good thing

                                 she got out" they say   softer   almost

"before the Russians   killed her"

                                                                      my child keeps

climbing unphased   longing   for summit   he welcomes

violence   wants a toy tank   knows   its caterpillar tracks crush not

butterfly wants arms arms   so many arms our bodies named

weapon   not wing or   is it the other way around   he climbs

arachnid *No*   *she left*   *before*   the older boy wants too   to clarify

make sure my son understands   the violence

in his bones   his mouth   his tongue   aloud bang   "There's a war there,

you know?   Right now!   They're killing

                                                  everyone!   Bombs!"

My son   looks down   from the top   or maybe sky   safe   *I know*

he says   *My mom was just*   *in a video*   *with some of them*   *doing poetry*

& stuff   how else   to end?

                                                  To go on

Dear Fellow Ukrainian Poet-Mama,

Because I cannot give you a child-caring robot
who will boil the marrow out of beef bones

to feed our sick children our great-grandmothers'
borsch because they were both named Vera

& wore their faith under their tongues because
they sang a dead language alive

because I do not know if our bloods
boiled beets in the same dead-sea

because the boiling point below
sea-level in your Odesa is lower

than my Dnieper riverland but now
we are both in sick elevation

red & drinking too much
tea & never enough vodka because

never enough is this country

we came to for too much of everything
& I remember my Vera would wear

black circles down her spine as proud
evil eyes left from cupping *this is how we know*

sickness has left the body she'd say
it leaves its dark mark but you & I

refuse such treatment & cough & carry
our sick under our clothes & hold

our children & take care of our sick spouses
& drink our tea & make wishes on loose

leaves at the bottoms of spent cups
because help doesn't come & in the morning

I'll text you a picture of wilted flowers
& the caption *parents feel dead inside* & we will laugh

about self-portraits & January

being years long & robots taking care of us
& I'll send you this poem & call it

sickness leaving its dark mark

The day after the longest day of the year

is longer & hotter & the sun
    rises as if it knows
        it will refuse to set
    & solstice is a lie
from an elsewhere
    language meaning
        "to stand still"
    when really
my son wakes
    with an urge
        to whirl & keep
    whirring knowing no
stillness & in a single
    day he has
        too many
    highest & lowest
points for even his own
    must-know-the-exact-
        count-of-everything
    brain to quantify
& I am crying in the car again
        with his little sister
    strapped in her car seat
the hour of daylight
    seems a whole-day long
        & she asks *Mama, please*
    play "Astronaut in the Ocean"
because it's big brother's
    favorite & he's not here

after his solar flare hands
struck my chest
the way meteors have pelleted
the moon for eons & she's
so used to being pocked
there's no pain
anymore just pressure & dent
we're underwater & I don't hold
my breath or breathe
& no I say to my daughter
trying to explain
another's sadness
to a three-year-old
who knows only
her own & screams
hot tears *I want "Astronaut
in the Ocean"* & the sun
turns liquid at the wheel
& I scream too & we're both
sobbing now the sun rising higher
& for an instant
through the windshield
glare & winding
mimosa blooms
Arkansas' unbearable heat
catches in cement
& the sun swims
still in the road ahead
& I give in & play

"*What you know*
about rollin' down
in the deep? . . ." & our tears
start to dry in all that wet
sunlight & she asks
Are you happy
now, Mama? & yes
I tell her I am
& when I come home
& for a split second
of radiant stillness
my son wraps hot
around me
I'll tell him *I am happy*
knowing the sun keeps burning
& he cannot stop
long enough to ask

Okean Means Endless

"It took the herd six hours,"
    the Blue Planet voice-over explains,
    orcas pushing a blue whale calf
under. *Keet*, our son points
at the screen, naming them all
one whale, from the greek *kētos*,
water-monster, "The seas bathed
in calf's blood." *More*, our son
asks. *More okean*, watches the red
beneath them spreading, *More ocean*.
"Killer whales," the voice reminds,
    the blue calf's heart bigger
than all three of ours, its blood could fill
our son's bathtub for weeks. The orcas
only eat the head, let the rest sink
to the ocean floor, but no, the voice
points out how body born six thousand pounds
lands on the skeleton of a full-grown blue,
"Nothing gets wasted in the water."
Look, our son staring. *Look,*
learning how the deep devours,
blubber separates from bone,
even bone won't survive long
eaten by water-worms and salt.
Spicy, our son calls any intense
flavor, tears in his mouth, but no,
not over this, the calf's
blood or its bones, the orcas
swimming through reddened salt,

but over desire, he wants
what he cannot have
or doesn't want what he is
given, a calf's heart
in the teeth of a hungrier mammal,
because what else is worth
that much salt?

Sour

Smell this, his father says, *has it gone bad?*
turned acid, give it time and it will always
lose sweet origin and thicken
with rot, *unlike me*, he says, *I was born
rotten*, something spoiled inside,
but milk, the stench of it
sticks in the nostrils like a child's
fat fingers, and this time, he didn't
fit our son's bottle lid on right,
so white poured out, all over
his thigh, pooled in his flip-flops,
and he tore the car door open, gagging
because more of it had lingered
inside, soured, spread
across the seats and floor, fogged
the windows rancid, *I can't stand
that smell*, he says, as though
a revelation, *something about it*, raised
on long-expired milk, my love's convinced
he deserves its rot, that all
along, it has been his, so now,
he won't get near the stuff,
now, he trusts nothing
in his parents' fridge, and when
our son broke out a rash so red
his cheeks looked bloodied, his father
knew he must have swallowed
too much curdle, knew too
that our son was not
born rotten.

V.

NITROGEN

Nitrogen is nitrogen, it passes miraculously from the air into plants, from these into animals, and from animals into us; when its function in our body is exhausted, we eliminate it, but it still remains nitrogen, aseptic, innocent.

—PRIMO LEVI

Why write another poem about the moon?

because my grays grow more numerous
than moonlight & when my son asks to pluck one

I tell him three more will shine
in its place because I do not tell him

about Hydra's serpent heads
multiplying this way because its teeth

raise skeletons from the dead
because my son already asks

where do the dead live?
with all their stones & stories

because he doesn't want me
to die *please please don't die*

he repeats *not ever* something
about other dead bodies must make

mine more certainly alive because the dog
is graying too so she will die soon he believes

& his Papa isn't much older but is sick & sleeps
a lot so he will die soon because *when I'm ten*

will you be very very old? he asks because
before he could say *moon* he loved her

in all her ageless light because he knew
she was stone & loved her all the more

for her undying heft
her float untethered

so when he plucks my grays
& begs the hairs *don't die* I let him

fall asleep their glowing strands
threaded around his fingers believing

this will keep me too

As Flesh, Not Stone

Remember, I tried. Not that this is any
consolation. Even now, writing it
feels like the opposite. I guess I'm referring
to distance. I tried to keep it
better than my mother or hers. Tried
to find the middle ground where your head
can meet my chest without being bound
or sinking. Where it can rest as flesh
not stone. Tried to keep that place
where our hands reach without touch,
to be okay with the empty space between.
—me water me me water me water me—
Remember the time I asked you to kiss me
and you said, *no Mama!* pushing my face away
with your hand's heel and then your foot's.
Remember how I listened. Let you choose
anything else over what you are made of.
—water me water me water water water—
Remember? The bathtub was only half full
when you slipped and asked me to kiss
your soapy earlobe so the pain would stop.
But it didn't. Not really. Remember, I tried.

Against Water

You refuse to let
    the lazy river take you, fight
        its current, holding tight
    to railings, walls, my outstretched arm, anything
to keep from following the flow.

        Salmon and steelhead swim
    upstream so their young survive
long enough to hatch, to fight
    for survival themselves.
        You have been fighting
    since birth. Against any water.
Doctors give us acronyms
    to name your urges. Pills
        to curb them. To help
    fit in they say.

Salmon and steelhead
    are the only fish to swim
        against the current, yet
we call them fish, loyal
to labels outside our species.
    You dunk another boy underwater
        in a game he called murderer, and you
    are named weird, strange, disturbed,
human, yes, but not quite.

Perhaps because an animal
        who stands out will get
eaten and soon go extinct.
Unless, that is, it turns
      its difference into strength.
          One fifth of all known fish
      populations are declining,
the salmon and steelheads
      mate and reproduce against
         the river's rush. They flood
      their scales and roe, iridescent,
the opposite direction
      of freshwater.

      They are surviving.

    You get knocked under
by the rush, emerge laughing, coughing, chlorine
      thick on your hair, knee
         scraped from the pool's
      hard bottom, red flesh
exposed like a gutted
      sockeye, eager
         to return to water.

Listening to Michael Jackson in a Closet

& on a kitchen floor & as a child & in our first
apartment several stops from DC & on the way
to the White House & in a bedroom of seven
refugees & as a daughter who brought
American music from Ukraine
back to America & as a mother
windows down blaring Billie Jean
through Ringgold Street in South
Philadelphia & in the bath drowning
deflated rubber ducks & when
the bubbles have left cloudy water
& my son demands *Alexa play*
Thriller & *Alexa volume 10* & *Alexa play it*
again louder & *play in English Alexa* & *does he*
really turn into a volk meaning wolf
& *Mama be a zombie* & *what's zombie*
in Russian? & *Mama play zombie tag*
& *Mama tantzui-dance* & *zhivi-live* & live
there's too much I cannot
translate but my son
can recognize Michael's voice
anywhere & *ABC easy*
as 123 & *that's the Jackson 5*
my American-born husband
corrects & *won't you please let me back*
in your heart & I grew up with Michael's voice
pushing the captive orca whale back
over a stone barricade & he pushed me
somewhere too so even as kids teased me

for loving Free Willy & sour cream &
& Michael & called me buffalo legs & smells-
of-garlic & voted me most likely
to be uncovered as an alien & asked if I was born
to like red & hammers & how we smuggled
our gold & how we hid our horns & how
we survived & I pressed play & play & play & play
on the cassette tape until
it unspooled & *it don't matter*
& Keiko never could have cleared
that height without *Carry me*
like you are my brother & love me
like a mother & will you be there? & my son
hear my song unspooling too
your body can music & robot
can moonwalk & break
free of any man-made or imagined
walls & listen to your feet my love
they sing across so many languages

Dear Sol'nishko, Little Sun,

November 7, 2020, the night before your fifth birthday

Remember, the city streets bloomed
human and I took your picture
jumping into a giant pile of leaves
where you buried your left shoe.
Remember, this was more than joy.
I don't want to find it, you said,
so you could walk half-barefoot,
bringing home November
on your sole and in your hair.
Remember how the air clung
to your heels, no earth
could hold you. Remember
my hands, even though
they have stopped trying
to ground your gravityless body,
remember they will always
reach to hold you. Remember,
you were born in the city
of brotherly love, in a country
of welcome, born from a foreign
people and tongue. Know, the day
you turned one, I lost faith
in love and in country. Remember,
even in loss, try to find hope
for joy. Know, tomorrow, the day
you turn five, there will be
dancing on Walnut, Chestnut,
Spruce, on every street
named tree. There will be

wishes and candles. Know
there will be sweetness.
It will be warm and the maples
will glow against our unseasonable
autumn, but no season is
as it was, my love. You will ask why
the trees are on fire and run
towards flame. You will dance,
always, and with the whole of you.
But know, while half the country
joins you in rejoice, the other
hates us for our joy. Remember,
anything born seed
has within itself the hope
to flower, cherry blossoms
along the tidal basin
clenched tighter than a fist
turn radiant bloom overnight.
Remember, you can choose
to believe in flight, the body's
weightlessness. Remember,
pressing your bare belly
into mine and saying this
is your favorite part, the soft
you came from. Remember joy
can be that soft, my love,
my fingers through your curls
as you fall asleep, joy
in every dry leaf they find.

AFTERGLOW

Two Years Later

The last thing I want is another poem
about war and dead children and how
we've forgotten their names.
My children are learning to count: bones

and wars and dead children and how
many days are left. *Now?* they ask, *now?*
My children are learning to count bones—
twenty-seven in the hand, twenty-two in the skull.

Many days are left now. They ask, *now?*
The last thing I want is to imagine them dead,
twenty-seven, twenty-two, their hands, their skulls.
I keep counting to make sure they're all there.

The last thing I want is to imagine the dead
we've forgotten. Their names,
I keep counting to make sure. They're all there.
The last thing I want is another poem.

You Ask to Count All the Stars

Even in a cloudless dark, in our small
swath of night, I tell you there are countless

we can't see. And in that smallness,
you lose track quick as dusk.

Clinging to Orion's belt, the little
and big bears, you give in to the human

way of flame-turned-animal
when distance is too great to name.

The blue ones, I tell you, are younger,
the red, older—dwarfs, planets, satellites.

What happens when they die? You ask.

How you already know the certainty
of endings. *They are so far*, I say,

their light is still making its way.
You telescope your eyes—full

moons of wonder. *They are forever
then*, your voice all answer & grown,

staring, starting—star
inside each eye, in every beginning.

ACKNOWLEDGMENTS

Thank you, reader, for making it through a difficult collection and now taking the time to learn about the many who helped make this book possible. And you among them, thank you for reading, feeling, and lingering within these pages.

Thank you to the following journals for giving these poems their first homes, sometimes as earlier versions: *The Account: A Journal of Poetry, Prose, and Thought*: "*Tell me it gets easier*," "When a friend texted to say her son's fish died & the child won't stop wailing," and "The day after the longest day of the year"; *American Poetry Review*: "Ferris Wheel"; *American Literary Review*: "On the 100th day of war in my birthplace:"; *Beloit Poetry Journal*: "I bring poets from Lviv, Ukraine, to my college class in Arkansas"; *Blackbird*: "It's not the dark"; *Bracken*: "Omen"; *Cleaver Magazine*: "As Flesh, Not Stone"; *The Common*: "What does the vulture say to the snowman(?) or how my son is learning to tell jokes(.)"; *Couplet Poetry*: "Why write another poem about the moon [with all her names] and [because my grays]"; *Diode*: "Sour"; *Flyway Journal*: "When my son says, *I don't love you*, I want to tell him about lilacs"; *Four Way Review*: "After the third snow day in a row, I'm ready to throw the towel"; *Frontier Poetry*: "Dear Sol'nishko, Little Sun" (published as "Letter to My Son"); *Greensboro Review*: "Am I a bad mother:"; *Hunger Mountains*: "Cataloguing Home, Dnipro to Little Rock"; *Ilanot Review*: "Hail"; *Iron Horse*: "Dear Fellow Ukrainian Poet-Mama [because I cannot]" (published as "Because I cannot give you a child-caring robot"); *The Main Review*: "Since becoming my son's only friend, I've had to become Baba Yaga."; *Missouri Review* online: "How many poems can I write about my son's insatiable longing?"; *Nashville Review*: "The Past Doesn't Rise Like Smoke" and "On Raising Mountains"; *Peste Magazine*: "Why write another poem about the moon [when every streak]"; *Poetry*: "I do not mention the war to my six-year-old son but somehow his body knows." and "*Okean* Means Endless"; *Poetry International*: "Listening to Michael Jackson in a Closet"; *Poetry Northwest*: "Why write another poem about the moon? [From earth]"; *Raleigh Review*: "Dear Fellow Ukrainian Poet-Mama [The tomatoes]" (published as "First Letter at the Beginning of the End"); *Rattle*, "Poets Respond": "One Year Later," "Two Years Later," and "The Ukrainian Flag Stares through the Balsam Fir from Larry's Farms"; *Shenandoah*: "Hurricane"; *Southern Humanities Review*: "Watching *Masha i Medved* as Russia Invades Ukraine" and "10 Months

Since the Full-Scale Invasion as Math Problem"; *SWWIM*: "Against Water"; and *Tahoma Literary Review*: "Why write another poem about the moon? [Mercury has two days]".

Immense gratitude to the University of Arkansas Press and Patricia Smith for believing in this book. Thank you to the whole editorial team for transforming these poems from files on a computer screen into the beautiful bound thing we can hold. Special gratitude to Janet Foxman for such attentive copyediting and William Clift for his work on the interior and exterior design.

Grateful to Arkhip for allowing us to use your powerful art for the cover while you continue to create in Kharkiv, under constant threat of violence. Thank you to the Ukrainian Cultural Association of Ohio for helping to organize the *Children of War* exhibit where I was introduced to this work.

Thank you to the Sustainable Arts Foundation, which believed in these poems and provided financial support that made this book possible.

With great appreciation to the Hendrix-Murphy Foundation and my colleagues at Hendrix College during the first part of writing this book.

Deep gratitude to Denison University and my colleagues here, who have quickly become dear friends, for your encouragement that allowed me to complete, revise, and submit this collection.

Thank you to my poetry teachers—Garrett Hongo, Geri Doran, and Michael Collier—for continuing to teach me well beyond the classroom.

To my dissertation advisors, Kevin M. F. Platt and Paul Saint-Amour, thank you for supporting my creative work alongside my scholarship.

Gratitude to the poets who have written the beautiful blurbs that grace this book—Ilya Kaminsky, Ellen Bass, and Oliver de la Paz—thank you for your generosity of spirit and time, for your thoughtful and tender words. Ilya, my Ukrainian-born kin, thank you for showing me what it is to carry our Slavic song into English and for using poetry to bring awareness and much-needed aid to our people. Ellen, without your faith in my first book, your care and encouragement, none of the next books would have followed. And Oliver, the neurodiversity panel we participated in together at AWP, as well as your own poems of parenthood, helped bring this book together.

Ross White, if it weren't for you, I'm not sure any of my poems would find their way to the page. Thank you for your friendship and unfaltering support.

To Luisa Muradyan, my dear fellow Ukrainian Poet-Mama, thank you for your friendship and constant readership, for knowing what it means to raise our children while powerlessly watching the children of our birthplace suffer. For your poems and person, which always give me humor and hope, always hope.

To the marvelous poets who have been generous enough to read and comment on versions of this whole manuscript—Kelly Grace Thomas, Donna Spruijt-Metz, and Minadora Macheret—I do not know what I did to deserve your keen eyes and ears, your fierce hearts, and most of all, your enduring friendship. And to the poets who have read numerous poems from the book and helped them find their final form or their way into the world, thank you for all the time you've spent with my words, for the care you've given each one that made the whole poem stronger: Adam Grabowski, Matt Kelsey-Garbutt, Keetje Kuipers, Olga Livshin, Erika Meitner, Tina Mozelle Braziel, and Dick Westheimer. Jehanne Dubrow, thank you for inspiring me with your villanelles. Kai Coggin, thank you for showing me how to fall in love with Arkansas, its landscape and people, the poetry of its community, unlike anywhere else. Christian, thank you for sharing our moon, for searching for her late into the night and always listening.

To my Columbus crew, I don't know what I would have done without you. Thank you for becoming family: Chelsea Bowden, Rachel Chilton, Candice Crilly, Craig Jendza, Jennifer Luebbers Leonard, Keith Leonard, Andrew McWard, and Adam Waterbury.

To my best friends forever from childhood, Anna Belopolskaya Koshi and Gina Belopolskaya, thank you for coming to my readings and sharing the longing for peace in our birthplace.

To my birthplace, Слава Україні!

To my parents, Svetlana and Michael, and my grandmother Rita, thank you for being the most dedicated grandparents and great-grandmother. You help make my career as a poet possible, now more than ever, by always being willing to take care of your grandchildren, so I can have more flexibility to travel and share poems about them with others.

And to my children, Valen and Remy—Val'ushka and Remichka—thank you for inspiring these poems and letting me write them. You are living, breathing poetry, and being a part of creating and raising you has been my greatest gift.